I0617035

MASTERING
DISCIPLINE
━◄ FOR SUCCESS ►━

A PRACTICAL GUIDE

BY: DR. CLEMENT KWAKYE

Copyright © 2024 Dr. Clement Kwakye

All Rights Reserved.

No part of this book may be reproduced, distributed, or transmitted in any form or by any means, including photocopying, recording, or other electronic or mechanical methods, without the prior written permission of the author, except in the case of brief quotations embodied in critical reviews and certain other non-commercial uses permitted by copyright law.

For permission requests, please contact the author at:
Email: Ckprofessionalconsulting@gmail.com

Disclaimer: The information in this book is provided for general informational purposes only. The author does not assume any responsibility or liability for any errors or omissions. The reader assumes full responsibility for the use of the information provided.

Welcome to a transformative journey that will unlock the power of self-discipline and take you to new heights of success. This isn't just another book filled with lofty theories or abstract ideas. It's a hands-on guide designed to help you break free from limiting habits, build unstoppable momentum, and achieve your goals—both big and small.

In these pages, we'll dive deep into the true meaning of discipline, revealing why it is the cornerstone of success in every area of life. You'll discover how self-discipline serves as the driving force behind personal growth, professional achievement, and long-term fulfillment. Whether you're striving to advance in your career, improve your health, or create lasting personal change, the principles you'll learn here will empower you to reach your full potential.

Together, we'll tackle some of the biggest roadblocks to success—procrastination, lack of focus, and wavering motivation. You'll gain powerful strategies to overcome these obstacles and build habits that will set you up for consistent progress. Through practical exercises, real-life examples, and actionable steps, you'll learn how to develop routines that align with your goals, set measurable targets, and stay on track even when challenges arise.

This journey isn't just about building self-control; it's about empowering you to take charge of your life. You'll learn how to:

- ➤ Conquer procrastination and develop laser-like focus.

- ➤ Master the art of setting and achieving meaningful goals.

- ➤ Build lasting habits that fuel success.

- ➤ Stay resilient and motivated, even in the face of setbacks.

By the end of this book, you won't just understand the theory of self-discipline—you'll have a personalized toolkit of strategies to apply in your everyday life. You'll have the confidence and clarity to tackle any challenge that comes your way, armed with the resilience to keep going no matter what. Whether you're looking to excel in your career, improve your personal life, or simply become the best version of yourself, this book will guide you every step of the way.

Prepare yourself for a life-changing experience. The road to success is paved with discipline, and now, it's time to take the first step. Let's get started!

TABLE OF CONTENTS

Chapter 1 Understanding Discipline And Its Importance 1

The Role of Discipline in Achieving Success.................................. 2

Common Myths About Discipline 3

Myth 1: Discipline Is an Innate Trait 3

Myth 2: Discipline Means Rigid Self-Denial 3

Myth 3: Discipline Requires Constant Willpower......................... 4

The Difference Between Motivation and Discipline 4

Discipline as a Tool for Managing Distractions and Temptations 6

The Empowering Nature of Discipline 7

Chapter 2 The Psychology of Self-Discipline 9

The Brain and Self-Discipline: How It Works 10

The Role of Willpower: Strengthening Your Inner Resolve 10

Triggers and Cues: Understanding and Managing Them........... 11

The Science of Habit Formation: Building Lasting Change......... 12

The Impact of Emotions on Self-Discipline 14

Self-Discipline and Identity: Becoming the Person You Want to Be
.... 15

Conclusion: The Psychological Foundation of Self-Discipline 16

Chapter 3 Setting Clear Goals for Focused Discipline 17

The Importance of SMART Goals 18

Breaking Down Large Goals into Manageable Steps 20

Visualization and Affirmations: Reinforcing Your Commitment 22

Creating a Roadmap for Success.. 24

Conclusion: The Power of Clear Goals in Self-Discipline 25

Chapter 4 Building Consistent Habits 27

The Power of Habits 28

The Science of Habit Formation... 28

Strategies for Building Consistent Habits 29

Overcoming Common Challenges in Habit Building 32

Conclusion: The Long-Term Impact of Consistent Habits 34

Chapter 5 Overcoming Procrastination 35

Understanding the Root Causes of Procrastination................... 36

The Impact of Procrastination on Discipline and Success.......... 38

Practical Strategies for Overcoming Procrastination 40

Conclusion: Taking Control of Procrastination 43

Chapter 6 Managing Distractions and Staying Focused................ 44

The Impact of Distractions on Productivity and Discipline 45

Common Sources of Distraction 45

Practical Strategies for Minimizing Distractions......................... 47

Building a Focused Mindset 50

Conclusion: The Power of Focus in Achieving Success 51

Chapter 7 Developing Mental Toughness 53

Understanding Mental Toughness 54

The Importance of Mental Toughness 55

Strategies for Developing Mental Toughness 57

Conclusion: The Journey to Mental Toughness 60

Chapter 8 Time Management and Prioritization 61

The Importance of Time Management 62

Time Management Techniques 63

Effective Prioritization 66

Conclusion: Mastering Time Management and Prioritization ... 69

Chapter 9 Sustaining Discipline Over the Long-Term 70

The Importance of Sustaining Discipline 71

Common Challenges in Sustaining Discipline 72

Strategies for Sustaining Discipline Over the Long Term 74

Conclusion: The Path to Lasting Success 76

Chapter 10 Creating a Personal Discipline Plan 78

The Purpose of a Personal Discipline Plan.................................. 79

Key Components of a Personal Discipline Plan 80

The Path to Sustained Success.. 84

Conclusion: The Journey to Mastery and Success Through Discipline... 85

The Foundation of Discipline 86

The Role of Psychology and Habit Formation 86

Overcoming Common Barriers: Procrastination and Distractions 87

Sustaining Discipline Over the Long Term 87

Time Management and Prioritization.. 88

Creating a Personal Discipline Plan... 88

The Power of Discipline in Achieving Success 89

Chapter 1: Understanding Discipline and Its Importance

- ➢ Definition of discipline
- ➢ The role of discipline in achieving success
- ➢ Differentiating between motivation and discipline
- ➢ Common myths about discipline

Chapter 2: The Psychology of Self-Discipline

- ➢ How the brain works in relation to habits and self-control
- ➢ The impact of willpower and how to strengthen it
- ➢ Understanding triggers and how to manage them
- ➢ The science behind forming new habits

Chapter 3: Setting Clear Goals for Focused Discipline

- ➢ The importance of setting SMART goals (Specific, Measurable, Achievable, Relevant, Time-bound)
- ➢ Breaking down large goals into manageable steps
- ➢ Creating a roadmap for success
- ➢ The role of visualization and affirmations in staying disciplined

Chapter 4: Building Consistent Habits

- ➢ The power of routine in developing discipline
- ➢ Step-by-step guide to creating new, positive habits
- ➢ The role of repetition in habit formation
- ➢ Overcoming common challenges in building habits

Chapter 5: Overcoming Procrastination

- ➢ Understanding why people procrastinate
- ➢ Techniques to overcome procrastination (e.g., Pomodoro Technique, time blocking)

- ➢ The relationship between procrastination and perfectionism
- ➢ Building momentum to stay on track

Chapter 6: Managing Distractions and Staying Focused

- ➢ Identifying and minimizing common distractions (digital and physical)
- ➢ Strategies for maintaining focus (e.g., mindfulness, deep work)
- ➢ The importance of creating an optimal environment for productivity
- ➢ Techniques for regaining focus when it's lost

Chapter 7: Developing Mental Toughness

- ➢ The role of resilience in maintaining discipline
- ➢ Techniques for building mental toughness (e.g., positive self-talk, embracing discomfort)
- ➢ The importance of a growth mindset
- ➢ Learning from setbacks and failures

Chapter 8: Time Management and Prioritization

- ➢ Understanding the relationship between time management and discipline
- ➢ Techniques for effective time management (e.g., Eisenhower Matrix, Pareto Principle)
- ➢ Prioritizing tasks to maximize productivity
- ➢ Balancing long-term goals with daily tasks

Chapter 9: Sustaining Discipline Over the Long Term

- ➢ Avoiding burnout and maintaining balance
- ➢ The importance of rest and recovery in sustaining discipline

> Tracking progress and celebrating small wins
> Staying motivated through long-term challenges

Chapter 10: Creating a Personal Discipline Plan

> Putting it all together: crafting your discipline plan
> Setting milestones and checkpoints
> Tools and resources to support your journey
> Staying accountable and adjusting your plan as needed

UNDERSTANDING DISCIPLINE AND ITS IMPORTANCE

Discipline is a concept that often evokes mixed feelings. On one hand, it is considered a vital component of success, the glue that holds the fabric of achievement together. On the other hand, it is often seen as challenging, demanding self-denial and rigorous control. However, the true essence of discipline is far more subtle and empowering than these extremes suggest. Understanding discipline and its importance is the first step toward harnessing its power to transform your life.

Discipline regulates behavior and actions to align with long-term goals and values, even when encountering distractions, temptations, or challenges. It involves making conscious decisions prioritizing one's future success over immediate gratification. This might sound simple, but in practice, it requires a deep understanding of one's motivations, consistent effort, and a willingness to embrace discomfort.

THE ROLE OF DISCIPLINE IN ACHIEVING SUCCESS

Discipline is often described as the bridge between goals and accomplishments. The steady, persistent force drives you to take action day after day, even when the initial excitement of a new goal has faded. Without discipline, even the most ambitious goals can become distant dreams as life's inevitable obstacles and setbacks diminish your motivation.

Consider any successful person in history—whether in business, sports, the arts, or personal development—and you will find that discipline is a common thread in their stories. Success is rarely a product of luck or raw talent; it results from disciplined effort over time. For example, a professional athlete may have natural talent, but without the discipline to train consistently, follow a strict diet, and recover properly, that talent will likely go to waste. Similarly, a successful entrepreneur may have a brilliant idea, but without the discipline to execute their vision, manage their time effectively, and stay focused on their goals, that idea may never come to fruition.

Discipline allows you to make progress, even when the path is difficult. It is the ability to keep moving forward when you're tired, faced with distractions, or when the rewards of your efforts are not immediately visible. This is why discipline is often more important than motivation. While motivation can provide a powerful initial push, discipline sustains you through the challenges and setbacks that inevitably arise on the journey to success.

One of the biggest obstacles to developing discipline is the prevalence of myths and misconceptions about what discipline is and how it works. These myths can create unrealistic expectations and discourage people from developing the discipline they need to achieve their goals. Let's explore some of the most common myths about discipline and the truths behind them.

MYTH 1: DISCIPLINE IS AN INNATE TRAIT

Many people believe that discipline is something you are born with or without—some people are naturally disciplined, while others are not. This belief can be discouraging because it suggests that if you struggle with discipline, you can do little to change that. However, this is far from the truth. Discipline is not a fixed trait but a skill that can be developed and strengthened over time. Building discipline requires practice, persistence, and a willingness to learn from mistakes, like learning a new language or creating a new physical skill. Anyone can become more disciplined with the right approach and mindset.

MYTH 2: DISCIPLINE MEANS RIGID SELF-DENIAL

Another common misconception is that discipline requires you to deny yourself any pleasure or enjoyment and to live a life of strict control and deprivation. This view of discipline can make it seem unappealing and unsustainable. In reality, discipline is not about denying yourself the things you enjoy; it's about making conscious choices that align with your long-term goals. This might mean saying no to certain temptations or distractions, but it also means creating a balanced life where you can enjoy your achievements and the process of working toward them. Proper discipline allows for flexibility and adaptation, recognizing that life is dynamic and that a rigid approach is neither necessary nor desirable.

MYTH 3: DISCIPLINE REQUIRES CONSTANT WILLPOWER

Many people think discipline is compatible with willpower and that discipline means constantly exerting effort to resist temptation. While willpower is undoubtedly a discipline component, relying solely on willpower is not sustainable. Willpower is a finite resource—it can be depleted by stress, fatigue, and decision-making. This is why disciplined people often focus on creating environments and routines that minimize the need for willpower. By developing habits and systems supporting their goals, they reduce the need to rely on willpower and constantly make disciplined behavior more automatic.

THE DIFFERENCE BETWEEN MOTIVATION AND DISCIPLINE

To truly understand the importance of discipline, it's essential to distinguish it from motivation. Motivation and discipline are often used interchangeably, but fundamentally different concepts play distinct roles in pursuing success.

Motivation is the emotional drive that inspires you to act. It excites you about a new goal or project and gives you the energy to start working toward it. Motivation is often triggered by external factors—such as a desire for recognition, the influence of others, or the appeal of a reward—or by internal factors like a personal passion or a sense of purpose.

However, motivation is inherently transient. It fluctuates based on your mood, circumstances, and the challenges you encounter. There will inevitably be days when you don't feel motivated, when the excitement of your goal has decreased, or obstacles make the path forward seem daunting. This is where discipline comes into play.

Discipline is the commitment to continue taking action toward your goals, regardless of your emotional state. It's the ability to push through resistance, boredom, or discomfort because you have decided to pursue a specific outcome. While motivation might get you started, discipline is what keeps you going. The steady, unwavering force ensures you continue to make progress, even when you don't feel particularly inspired.

Understanding this distinction is crucial because it highlights the limitations of relying on motivation alone. Many people set ambitious goals and start with high motivation levels, only to lose momentum when that initial burst of enthusiasm fades. With discipline, staying within your goals is easy when the going gets tough. By recognizing that discipline is a skill that can be developed, you can learn to maintain consistent progress, even when motivation is low.

In today's world, distractions are everywhere. From the constant ping of notifications on your phone to the endless stream of online content, countless things compete for your attention at any moment. These distractions can quickly disrupt your progress, challenging your ability to stay focused on your goals. This is where discipline becomes a powerful tool.

Discipline helps you to manage distractions by creating boundaries and prioritizing your time and energy. It allows you to make conscious choices about where you focus your attention and to resist the pull of immediate gratification in favor of long-term success. For example, if you're trying to build a business, discipline might involve setting specific times for checking emails or social media rather than allowing these activities to interrupt your work throughout the day. Establishing routines and habits that minimize distractions creates an environment where disciplined behavior becomes the default.

Temptations, like distractions, are another significant challenge for discipline. Whether it's the temptation to indulge in unhealthy foods while trying to maintain a diet, to skip a workout when you're tired, or to procrastinate on an important task, temptations can lead you off course and undermine your progress. Discipline allows you to resist these temptations and stay true to your goals.

It's important to note that discipline doesn't mean denying yourself pleasure entirely; instead, it's about making intentional choices that align with your long-term objectives. This might mean indulging in a treat occasionally but doing so in a way that doesn't disrupt your overall progress. Over time, as you develop discipline, you'll find that resisting temptations becomes more accessible, and you'll experience the satisfaction of making choices that support your success.

THE EMPOWERING NATURE OF DISCIPLINE

One of the most significant benefits of discipline is its sense of empowerment. When you develop discipline, you control your life and destiny. You are no longer at the mercy of external circumstances or fleeting emotions; instead, you are guided by a clear sense of purpose and the knowledge that you can achieve your goals.

This empowerment extends beyond just achieving specific objectives. Discipline fosters a sense of self-respect and confidence. When you consistently make disciplined choices, you build trust in yourself and your abilities. You prove you can set goals and follow through, even when difficult. This self-trust is invaluable and can have a positive ripple effect on all areas of your life.

Understanding discipline and its importance is the foundation for success. Discipline is not about rigid control or constant self-denial; it's about making conscious, intentional choices that align with your long-term goals. By developing discipline, you can navigate distractions, overcome temptations, and consistently progress toward your aspirations. In the following chapters, we will explore practical strategies and techniques to help you cultivate and sustain discipline, enabling you to unlock your full potential and achieve your desired success.

2

THE PSYCHOLOGY OF SELF-DISCIPLINE

Self-discipline is not merely a matter of willpower or sheer determination. It is deeply rooted in the psychology of thinking, feeling, and acting. Understanding self-discipline's psychological mechanisms can empower you to cultivate and maintain it more effectively. In this chapter, we will explore the inner workings of self-discipline, including how the brain operates through habits and self-control, the role of willpower, the impact of triggers and cues, and the science behind forming new habits.

To grasp how self-discipline functions, it's essential to understand the brain's role in regulating behavior. The prefrontal cortex, the brain area responsible for decision-making, planning, and impulse control, plays a critical role in self-discipline. This part of the brain is like a muscle—its strength and effectiveness can be developed with practice, but it also has limits.

When you exercise self-discipline, you engage the prefrontal cortex to override more primitive brain structures, such as the limbic system, which is responsible for our emotions and desires. The limbic system drives us toward immediate gratification—seeking pleasure and avoiding pain. In contrast, the prefrontal cortex allows us to think about the future, weigh the consequences of our actions, and choose behaviors that align with our long-term goals.

However, the prefrontal cortex has a finite capacity for self-control. When we face daily decisions, especially those requiring resisting temptations or making difficult choices, this part of the brain can become fatigued. This phenomenon is known as "decision fatigue," it explains why people often struggle with self-discipline later in the day or after making numerous decisions. Understanding this can help you plan your day more effectively, placing tasks that require high levels of discipline earlier in the day when your prefrontal cortex is freshest.

Willpower is often thought of as the driving force behind self-discipline. Mental energy allows us to resist temptations and focus on our goals. However, like any form of energy, willpower can be depleted. When you use willpower to resist temptation or push through a challenging task, you draw on a limited resource. This is why maintaining self-discipline can be difficult when you are tired, stressed, or overwhelmed.

Psychologist Roy Baumeister, a leading researcher in self-control, has compared willpower to muscle. As a muscle gets tired after exertion, so does willpower after prolonged use. However, like a muscle, willpower can be strengthened with practice. Regularly engaging in activities that require self-control, such as sticking to a schedule, resisting small temptations, or setting and following through on daily goals, can gradually increase your willpower reserves.

Moreover, research suggests that your beliefs about willpower can influence how you use it. People who believe willpower is a finite resource that depletes quickly are likelier to experience willpower depletion. In contrast, those who think that willpower is something they can replenish are better able to maintain self-discipline even after a challenging day. This indicates that cultivating a mindset that views willpower as renewable and resilient can help you enhance self-discipline.

TRIGGERS AND CUES: UNDERSTANDING AND MANAGING THEM

Our environments are filled with triggers and cues that influence our behavior, often without us being fully aware of their impact. A trigger or cue is any stimulus—such as a time of day, a specific location, or even an emotional state—that prompts a particular behavior. For instance, the sight of a snack might trigger the urge to eat, even if you're not hungry, or checking your phone could trigger a habit of mindlessly scrolling through social media.

Understanding the triggers that influence your behavior is crucial for developing self-discipline. By identifying the specific cues that lead to undesired behaviors, you can take steps to manage them. For example, if you know you tend to procrastinate when working in a cluttered environment, you can improve your self-discipline by tidying up your workspace. Similarly, if you tend to overeat when you're stressed, you can work on developing healthier stress-management techniques.

One effective strategy for managing triggers is to create "if-then" plans, also known as implementation intentions. This involves identifying a specific trigger and planning a desired response. For example, if you know that you tend to skip your workout when you're tired, you might create a plan that says, "If I feel tired after work, then I will still go to the gym for at least 10 minutes." By pre-committing to a response, you reduce the cognitive load of deciding at the moment, making it easier to stick to your goals.

THE SCIENCE OF HABIT FORMATION: BUILDING LASTING CHANGE

Habits are the foundation of self-discipline. They are behaviors that have become automatic, requiring little conscious effort or willpower. Understanding the science behind habit formation can help you build new, positive habits and break old, negative ones.

The process of habit formation is often described as a "habit loop," which consists of three main components: the cue, the routine, and the reward. The cue is the trigger that initiates the behavior, the routine is the behavior itself, and the reward is the positive reinforcement that follows the behavior. For example, if your cue is feeling stressed, your routine might be to eat a snack, and your reward is the temporary relief from stress that eating provides.

You must identify these three components to create a new habit and consciously design your habit loop. Start by choosing a cue that will consistently trigger your desired behavior. This could be something as simple as a time of day, a specific location, or an emotional state. Next, decide on a routine—an action that you can repeat regularly. Finally, reward yourself for completing the routine, even if the reward is small. This reinforces the behavior and helps to cement the habit.

One critical insight from habit research is that repetition is crucial. The more you repeat a behavior responding to a specific cue, the more automatic it becomes. Over time, the neural pathways associated with the habit become more robust, and the behavior requires less conscious effort. This is why consistency is so important when developing new habits.

However, breaking a bad habit can be more challenging because it often involves disrupting an established habit loop. To break a bad habit, you must identify triggers and replace the routine with different, healthier behaviors. For example, if you habitually check your phone first thing in the morning, you might replace that routine with a few minutes of meditation or stretching. The key is to find a replacement behavior that provides a similar reward, making it easier to stick with the change.

Emotions play a significant role in self-discipline, often catalyzing or an obstacle to disciplined behavior. Positive emotions, such as a sense of accomplishment or pride in your progress, can reinforce self-discipline by rewarding your goals. On the other hand, negative emotions, such as stress, anxiety, or frustration, can undermine self-discipline by triggering behaviors that provide short-term relief but are counterproductive in the long run.

Managing your emotions effectively is crucial for maintaining self-discipline. One effective technique is emotional regulation, which involves recognizing and managing your emotional responses in a way that supports your goals. This might include mindfulness, deep breathing, or cognitive reframing—changing how you interpret and respond to a situation.

For example, if you feel overwhelmed by a large project, you might be tempted to procrastinate to avoid discomfort. However, practicing mindfulness allows you to observe your emotions without letting them dictate your behavior. Instead of avoiding the task, you might break it down into smaller, more manageable steps, reducing the feeling of overwhelm and making it easier to get started.

Another critical aspect of emotional regulation is developing resilience—the ability to bounce back from setbacks and keep moving forward. Resilience is closely linked to self-discipline because it helps you maintain your commitment to your goals even when encountering difficulties. Cultivating a growth mindset, where you view challenges as opportunities for learning and growth, can enhance your resilience and, by extension, your self-discipline.

One of the most powerful ways to develop self-discipline is to align
it with your identity—how you see yourself and who you aspire to
become. When you view self-discipline as an integral part of your
identity, it becomes easier to make disciplined choices because they
are consistent with how you see yourself.

For example, if you see yourself as a healthy and active person, it
becomes easier to make disciplined choices around diet and
exercise because those behaviors align with your identity. Similarly,
if you see yourself as diligent and hardworking, you are more likely
to stick to your work commitments and push through challenges.

One way to align self-discipline with your identity is to use
affirmations or self-statements reinforcing your desired identity.
For example, instead of saying, "I need to exercise more," you might
say, "I am someone who prioritizes my health and well-being." By
framing self-discipline as part of your identity, you create a positive

feedback loop where disciplined behavior reinforces your self-image, and your self-image, in turn, reinforces disciplined behavior.

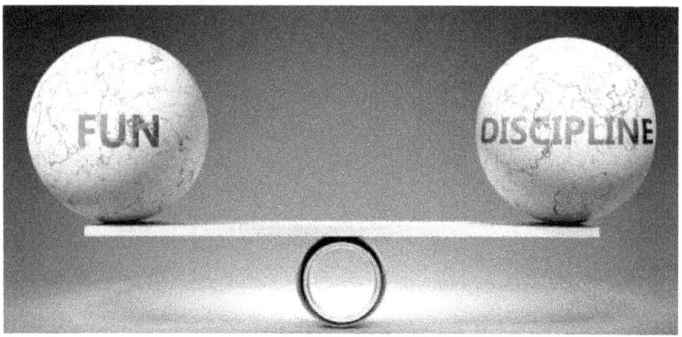

CONCLUSION: THE PSYCHOLOGICAL FOUNDATION OF SELF-DISCIPLINE

CONCLUSION: THE PSYCHOLOGICAL FOUNDATION OF SELF-DISCIPLINE

Self-discipline is not just about exerting control over your behavior; it is about understanding the psychological processes that drive your actions and learning how to manage them effectively. By understanding the role of the brain, the impact of willpower, the influence of triggers and cues, and the science of habit formation, you can develop strategies that enhance your self-discipline and make it easier to achieve your goals. Moreover, you can create a solid psychological foundation for lasting change by managing your emotions and aligning self-discipline with your identity.

In the next chapter, we will explore practical strategies for setting clear goals to be the foundation for your self-discipline journey. These strategies will help you create a roadmap for success, ensuring that your efforts are focused and aligned with your long-term aspirations.

3

SETTING CLEAR GOALS FOR FOCUSED DISCIPLINE

Setting clear goals is a crucial step in developing and maintaining self discipline. Without well-defined goals, it's easy to become distracted, lose motivation, and ultimately drift away from the actions necessary for success. Clear goals provide direction and purpose, acting as a roadmap that guides your daily decisions and behaviors. This chapter explores the importance of setting specific, measurable, achievable, relevant, and time-bound (SMART) goals, breaking down significant goals into manageable steps, and how visualization and affirmations can reinforce your commitment to these goals.

One of the most effective ways to set clear goals is using the SMART criteria, which stands for Specific, Measurable, Achievable, Relevant, and Time-bound. This framework helps ensure your goals are clear, realistic, and actionable, providing a solid foundation for disciplined effort.

1. **Specific**: A goal must be specific enough to give you clear directions. Vague goals like "get in shape" or "improve my career" lack the clarity to create an actionable plan. Instead, a specific goal such as "lose 10 pounds by exercising four times a week and eating a balanced diet" or "earn a promotion by completing a professional certification and taking on new responsibilities at work" gives you a clear target to aim for. Specificity helps you understand exactly what you need to do, making it easier to stay disciplined.

2. **Measurable**: A measurable goal allows you to track your progress and stay motivated. When you can measure your progress, you know whether you're on track or need to adjust your efforts. For example, if your goal is to save money, setting a measurable goal like "save $5,000 in the next six months" gives you a clear benchmark against which to measure. Tracking your progress provides a sense of achievement, reinforcing your discipline and keeping you focused on your goal.

3. **Achievable**: Setting ambitious goals is essential but should also be realistic and attainable. Setting a goal that is too far out of reach can lead to frustration and a loss of motivation. On the other hand, a goal that is too easy to achieve might need to provide more challenges to keep you engaged. Achievable goals balance ambition and realism,

encouraging you to push yourself while remaining within the realm of possibility. For example, if you're currently running 5 miles a week, setting a marathon goal in three months might be unrealistic, but aiming to run 10 miles a week within the next month is more achievable

4. **Relevant**: Your goals should be aligned with your broader life objectives and values. An appropriate goal matters to you and is connected to a larger purpose. This relevance motivates you to stay disciplined, especially when challenges arise. For example, if your long-term goal is to advance in your career, a relevant short-term goal might be to network with industry professionals or to develop a new skill that is in demand in your field. Ensuring your relevant goals helps you prioritize your efforts and stay committed to your long-term vision.

5. **Time-bound**: Every goal should have a deadline or a timeframe. A time-bound goal creates a sense of urgency and helps you stay focused. Without a deadline, it's easy to procrastinate or become complacent. For example, instead of setting a goal to "read more books," you might set a time-bound goal to "read 12 books by the end of the year." Having a deadline keeps you accountable and encourages you to take consistent action.

Setting SMART goals creates a clear and actionable plan essential for disciplined progress. Each element of the SMART framework works together to ensure your goals are well-defined and aligned with your long-term aspirations.

One of the biggest challenges in staying disciplined is managing significant, daunting goals. When faced with an overwhelming goal, it's easy to become discouraged and lose focus. It's essential to break down significant goals into smaller, manageable steps to overcome this. This process makes your goals more achievable and helps you maintain momentum and stay motivated.

1. **Start with the End in Mind**: Clearly define your long-term goal. What outcome do you want to achieve? For example, if your goal is to write a book, your long-term objective might be to complete a 300-page manuscript. Once you have a clear vision of your end goal, you can work backward to identify the steps needed.

2. **Divide the Goal into Milestones**: Break your long-term goal into smaller milestones, each representing a significant step toward your ultimate objective. For example, if your goal is to write a book, you might set milestones such as completing the outline, writing the first draft of each

chapter, revising the manuscript, and submitting the final draft. These milestones give you clear targets to aim for and help you measure your progress.

3. **Create Actionable Tasks**: Once you've identified your milestones, break them into specific, actionable tasks. For example, if your milestone is to complete the outline of your book, your tasks include brainstorming ideas, researching your topic, and drafting an outline for each chapter. By breaking milestones into smaller tasks, you create a clear and manageable plan for achieving your goal.

4. **Prioritize and Schedule Tasks**: With your actionable tasks identified, prioritize them based on their importance and urgency. Then, schedule them into your daily or weekly routine. By assigning specific deadlines to each task, you create a sense of accountability and ensure that you stay on track. For example, set a goal to complete your book outline within two weeks, scheduling time each day to work on different sections.

5. **Review and Adjust**: Review your progress regularly and plan as needed. If you're falling behind on specific tasks, reassess your schedule and make the necessary adjustments. Flexibility is crucial in maintaining discipline, allowing you to adapt to challenges and focus on your goal.

Breaking down significant goals into manageable steps makes the process more manageable and achievable. Focusing on one step at a time can maintain momentum and build confidence as you move closer to your ultimate objective.

Visualization and affirmations are powerful tools that can help reinforce your commitment to your goals and enhance your self-discipline. These techniques involve mentally rehearsing your success and using positive self-talk to stay motivated and focused.

1. **The Power of Visualization**: Visualization creates a mental image of your desired outcome. By vividly imagining yourself achieving your goal, you develop a sense of familiarity and confidence that can help you stay disciplined. For example, if you want to run a marathon, you might visualize yourself crossing the finish line, feeling strong and accomplished. This mental rehearsal helps to condition your mind for success, making it easier to stay focused and motivated.

Find a quiet place to relax and close your eyes to practice visualization. Begin by imagining your goal in as much detail as possible. What does success look like? How does it feel? Engage all your senses to make the experience as accurate as possible. The more vividly you can imagine your success, the more influential the impact will be on your mindset and behavior.

2. **Using Affirmations**: Affirmations are positive statements that reinforce your belief in your ability to achieve your goals. Repeating affirmations can reprogram your subconscious to support your efforts and enhance self-discipline. For example, if your goal is to improve your health, you might use affirmations like "I am strong and capable of making healthy choices" or "I am committed to my health and well-being."

Affirmations must be used consistently and with conviction to be effective. Choose affirmations that resonate with you and reflect your goals. Repeat them daily, preferably in the morning or before bed, to set a positive tone for your day or reinforce your commitment as you wind down. Over time, these affirmations can help shift your mindset and make disciplined behavior more natural and automatic.

3. **Combining Visualization and Affirmations**: For maximum impact, combine visualization and affirmations into a single practice. As you visualize your success, incorporate your affirmations to reinforce your belief in your ability to achieve your goals. For example, as you visualize yourself completing a significant project, you might repeat affirmations like "I am focused and disciplined in my work" or "I am capable of achieving great things."

By consistently practicing visualization and affirmations, you can create a robust mental framework that supports your goals and enhances your self-discipline. These techniques help to keep your mind focused on your desired outcome, making it easier to stay committed to the actions necessary for success.

Setting clear goals is just the first step in your journey toward success. To ensure that you stay on track and maintain discipline, it's essential to create a detailed roadmap that outlines the steps you need to take to achieve your goals. This roadmap serves as a guide, helping you navigate the challenges and obstacles that will inevitably arise.

1. **Start with Your Long-Term Vision**: Begin by clearly defining your long-term vision. What goal do you want to achieve? This could be a career aspiration, a personal achievement, or a significant life change. Write down your vision in as much detail as possible and keep it somewhere visible as a constant reminder of what you're working toward.

2. **Set SMART Goals**: Using the SMART criteria, set specific, measurable, achievable, relevant, and time-bound goals that align with your long-term vision. Break down each goal

into smaller milestones and actionable tasks and prioritize them based on their importance and urgency.

3. **Create a Timeline**: Develop a timeline that outlines the steps you need to take to achieve your goals. Assign specific deadlines to each task and milestone, and schedule them into your daily or weekly routine. Be realistic about the time and effort required and build some flexibility to account for unexpected challenges.

4. **Track Your Progress**: Review your progress regularly and adjust your roadmap. Use a journal, planner, or digital tool to track your achievements and reflect on your journey. Celebrate your successes, no matter how small, and use any setbacks as opportunities to learn and grow.

5. **Stay Accountable**: Share your goals with a trusted friend, mentor, or coach who can support and hold you accountable. Regular check-ins can help keep you motivated and ensure that you stay on track.

Creating a roadmap for success helps to translate your goals into actionable steps, making it easier to maintain discipline and stay focused on your objectives. With a clear plan, you can approach each day purposefully and confidently, knowing you are steadily moving closer to your desired outcome.

CONCLUSION: THE POWER OF CLEAR GOALS IN SELF - DISCIPLINE

Clear goals are the foundation of self-discipline. They provide direction, purpose, and motivation, helping you stay focused and committed to your long-term vision. By setting SMART goals, breaking them down into manageable steps, and using visualization and affirmations to reinforce your commitment, you can create a robust roadmap for success.

The next chapter will explore building consistent habits essential for maintaining self-discipline over the long term. By turning disciplined behavior into a habit, you can progress toward your goals with greater ease and consistency, ultimately leading to lasting success.

4

BUILDING CONSISTENT HABITS

Habits are the foundation of self-discipline. They are the small, often unconscious actions that shape our lives and determine our success. When habits align with our goals, they become powerful tools that drive consistent progress, making discipline almost effortless. In contrast, when our habits are misaligned with our aspirations, they can act as obstacles, hindering our progress and leading us astray. In this chapter, we will delve into the science of habit formation, explore strategies for building consistent habits, and discuss how to overcome common challenges in the habit-building process.

Habits are automatic behaviors that we perform with little conscious thought. They are the brain's way of conserving energy, allowing us to carry out routine tasks efficiently. For instance, brushing your teeth, driving to work, or checking your email are all habits that have become ingrained through repetition. These behaviors are triggered by specific cues and followed by a routine that delivers a reward, completing what is known as the "habit loop."

The power of habits lies in their ability to shape our lives over time. While a single action may seem insignificant, the cumulative effect of repeated behaviors can be profound. For example, consistently exercising 30 minutes a day may seem like little, but it can significantly improve health and fitness over time. Similarly, the habit of setting aside a portion of your income for savings can, over the years, result in substantial financial security.

Because habits operate mainly on autopilot, they free up mental resources for more complex decision-making. This makes them incredibly valuable in maintaining self-discipline, as they reduce the need for constant willpower and decision-making. Once a positive habit is established, staying on track toward your goals becomes more accessible because the behavior requires less effort and conscious thought.

THE SCIENCE OF HABIT FORMATION

To build consistent habits, it's essential to understand the science behind how habits are formed. Habits are created through a process that involves three key components: the cue, the routine, and the reward. This cycle, known as the habit loop, is the foundation of all habitual behavior.

1. **The Cue**: The cue is the trigger that initiates the habit. It can be anything from a specific time of day, an emotional state, a particular location, or an external event. For example, the sound of your alarm clock in the morning might cue the habit of getting out of bed and starting your day. The key to building a habit is identifying and establishing consistent cues to trigger the desired behavior.

2. **The Routine**: The routine is the behavior—the action you want to turn into a habit. This could be something like exercising, reading, or practicing a skill. Routine is the most visible part of the habit loop, and you actively work on it during the habit-building process. Repetition is crucial here; the more you repeat the routine in response to the cue, the more ingrained the habit becomes.

3. **The Reward**: The reward is the positive reinforcement that follows the routine. It's what makes the behavior satisfying and encourages you to repeat it in the future. Rewards can be intrinsic, like the feeling of accomplishment after completing a task, or extrinsic, like a treat or a break. Identifying a meaningful reward is essential for solidifying the habit, as it helps your brain associate the routine with a positive outcome.

STRATEGIES FOR BUILDING CONSISTENT HABITS

Building consistent habits requires deliberate effort and a strategic approach. Here are several strategies that can help you establish and maintain positive habits:

1. **Start Small**: One of the most common mistakes people make when building new habits is starting too big. Setting overly ambitious goals can lead to frustration and burnout,

making it challenging to stick with the habit. Instead, start with a miniature, manageable version of the habit. For example, if your goal is to build a habit of daily exercise, start with just five minutes a day. Once this becomes easy and automatic, gradually increases the duration. Starting small creates a sense of accomplishment and builds momentum, making it easier to sustain the habit over time.

2. **Anchor Habits to Existing Routines**: One of the most effective ways to establish a new habit is to anchor it to an existing routine. This is known as "habit stacking." The idea is to identify a habit you already do consistently and attach the new habit to it. For example, if you want to build a habit of flossing your teeth, you might stack it onto your existing habit of brushing your teeth. Every time you finish brushing, you immediately floss. You create a strong cue that triggers the desired behavior by linking the new habit to a well-established routine.

3. **Use Environmental Cues**: Your environment plays a significant role in shaping your habits. Designing your environment to support your goals can make building and maintaining positive habits easier. For example, if you want to build a habit of eating healthier, you can stock your kitchen with nutritious foods and remove unhealthy options. To develop a reading habit, keep books in visible, easily accessible locations around your home. The more you can align your environment with your desired habits, the more likely you will succeed.

4. **Commit to Consistency**: Consistency is key to habit formation. The more consistently you perform a behavior, the stronger the habit becomes. Even if the habit is small or

the effort minimal, what matters most is that you do it regularly. To build consistency, commit to practicing the habit every day, even just for a few minutes. Over time, this consistency will help the habit become automatic, reducing the need for conscious effort.

5. **Track Your Progress**: Tracking your progress can be a powerful motivator and reinforcement tool. Whether you use a journal, an app, or a simple checklist, tracking lets you see how far you've come and keeps you accountable. It also provides a visual reminder of your commitment to the habit, making it harder to skip a day. Additionally, tracking can help you identify patterns and obstacles hindering your progress, allowing you to make adjustments as needed.

6. **Plan for Obstacles**: No habit-building journey is without challenges. To maintain consistency, it's important to anticipate potential obstacles and plan for them in advance. This could include identifying situations that might disrupt your routine, such as travel, busy schedules, or unexpected events, and developing strategies to stay on track. For example, if you're trying to build a habit of exercising, you might plan for a shorter workout on hectic days or find alternative ways to stay active, such as taking the stairs instead of the elevator. Planning for obstacles increases your chances of maintaining the habit even when life gets in the way.

7. **Celebrate Small Wins**: Celebrating small wins can boost your motivation and reinforce your commitment to the habit. Every time you successfully perform the habit, no matter how small, take a moment to acknowledge your achievement. This could be as simple as giving yourself a

mental pat on the back, treating yourself to a small reward, or sharing your progress with a friend. Celebrating small wins helps to create positive associations with the habit, making it more enjoyable and sustainable over time.

OVERCOMING COMMON CHALLENGES IN HABIT BUILDING

While building consistent habits is critical to long-term success, it's not without its challenges. Understanding how to address these challenges can help you stay on track and maintain your commitment to your goals.

- **The Plateau Effect**: One of the most common challenges in habit building is the plateau effect. This occurs when you stop seeing progress after an initial improvement period, leading to frustration and a potential loss of motivation. To overcome this, it's essential to recognize that plateaus are a natural part of the habit-building process. Progress often occurs in waves, with periods of rapid improvement followed by slower growth. During a plateau, focus on maintaining consistency rather than seeking immediate results. Trust that your efforts build a strong foundation, even if the progress isn't immediately visible.

- **Lack of Immediate Rewards**: Many habits, especially those related to long-term goals, need to provide immediate rewards. For example, the benefits of exercising, saving money, or learning a new skill often take time to manifest. This can make it challenging to stay motivated and consistent. To address this, creating short-term rewards that keep you engaged is helpful. For example, reward yourself with a relaxing bath or a favorite healthy snack after completing a workout. These small rewards provide immediate satisfaction and help bridge the gap between effort and long-term rewards.

- **All-or-nothing Thinking**: All-or-nothing thinking can significantly hinder building consistent habits. This mindset leads you to believe it's not worth doing if you can't do something perfectly or stick to your habit 100% of the time. This can result in giving up entirely after a single slip-up or missed day. To overcome this, embrace the concept of "progress, not perfection." Recognize that building a habit is a journey, and setbacks are a normal part of the process. Instead of focusing on perfection, aim for consistency and resilience. If you miss a day or make a mistake, don't dwell on it—get back on track as soon as possible.

- **Overconfidence and Complacency**: Once a habit becomes established, it's easy to become overconfident and complacent, assuming the habit will continue without effort. However, habits, like muscles, require ongoing maintenance to stay strong. To avoid complacency, regularly assess your habits and make adjustments as needed. This might involve setting new goals, increasing the difficulty of the habit, or finding new ways to challenge yourself. By staying engaged and committed, you can ensure that your habits continue to support your long-term success.

Building consistent habits is one of the most effective ways to maintain self-discipline and achieve long-term success. Habits provide the structure and routine needed to stay focused on your goals, reducing the need for constant willpower and decision-making. By understanding the science of habit formation, implementing effective strategies, and overcoming common challenges, you can establish positive habits that align with your aspirations and drive consistent progress.

In the next chapter, we will explore overcoming procrastination, another common barrier to self-discipline and success. By understanding the root causes of procrastination and developing strategies to address it, you can further enhance your ability to stay focused and disciplined in pursuing your goals.

5

OVERCOMING PROCRASTINATION

Procrastination is a challenge that many people face when trying to achieve their goals and maintain discipline. It's the tendency to delay essential tasks, often in favor of more pleasurable or less demanding activities, even when you know that postponing will result in negative consequences. Overcoming procrastination is necessary for anyone striving to succeed, as it can be one of the most significant barriers to consistent progress. In this chapter, we will explore the root causes of procrastination, discuss its impact on discipline and success, and provide practical strategies to overcome it.

Procrastination is a complex behavior with multiple underlying causes. It's not simply a matter of laziness or poor time management; rather, it often stems from deeper psychological and emotional factors. Understanding these root causes is crucial for effectively addressing procrastination.

1. **Fear of Failure**: One of the most common reasons for procrastination is the fear of failure. When you fear that you might fail in a task, you might delay starting it to avoid the possibility of failure. This fear can be paralyzing, leading to a cycle of procrastination where the longer you put off the task, the more intimidating it becomes. This fear is often rooted in perfectionism, where the individual feels that anything less than perfect is unacceptable. To overcome this, it's essential to recognize that failure is a natural part of the learning process and that making mistakes is a valuable opportunity for growth.

2. **Perfectionism**: Perfectionism is closely related to the fear of failure. Perfectionists often set unrealistically high standards for themselves, which can lead to procrastination. They may delay starting a task because they are waiting for the perfect conditions or are afraid they won't be able to meet their expectations. Perfectionism can create a sense of overwhelm, making it difficult to take the first step. Overcoming perfectionism involves accepting that perfection is unattainable, and that progress is more important than perfection.

3. **Lack of Motivation**: Sometimes, procrastination occurs simply because the task could be more enjoyable. When

you lack motivation, it's easy to prioritize other activities that provide more immediate gratification. Disconnection between the task and your long-term goals or values can exacerbate this lack of motivation. To address this, it's essential to find ways to connect the task to something that matters to you, whether it's a larger goal, personal value, or a sense of purpose.

4. **Overwhelming and Anxiety**: Feeling overwhelmed by the size or complexity of a task can lead to procrastination. When a task seems too daunting, you might delay starting it because you don't know where to begin or because tackling it feels too stressful. This overwhelm can lead to anxiety, which further reinforces procrastination. Breaking the task down into smaller, more manageable steps can help reduce the feeling of overwhelm and make it easier to get started.

5. **Lack of Structure and Time Management**: Procrastination can also result from poor time management and structure. With a clear plan or schedule, keeping track of time and prioritizing less important activities over critical tasks is more accessible. This lack of structure can lead to disorganization, making it difficult to focus on what needs to be done. Effective time management strategies, such as blocking or creating to-do lists, provide the necessary structure to overcome procrastination.

Procrastination significantly impacts discipline and, ultimately, your ability to achieve success. When you procrastinate, you undermine your self-discipline by allowing short-term impulses to override long-term goals. This can create a negative cycle where procrastination leads to feelings of guilt, stress, and frustration, which in turn makes it even harder to stay disciplined and focused.

1. **Erosion of Self-Confidence**: Procrastination can reduce self-confidence, as repeated delays and missed deadlines lead to feelings of inadequacy and self-doubt. When you consistently fail to meet your commitments, you question your abilities and worth, diminishing your motivation and discipline. This erosion of self-confidence can create a self-fulfilling prophecy where you avoid tasks because you don't believe you can succeed, and as a result, you don't make progress.

2. **Increased Stress and Anxiety**: Procrastination often increases stress and anxiety as deadlines loom and tasks

pile up. The pressure of knowing that you have a lot of work to do but little time to do it can be overwhelming, leading to a cycle of stress that makes it even harder to concentrate and be productive. This stress can hurt your mental and physical health, hindering your ability to stay disciplined.

3. **Missed Opportunities**: Procrastination can result in missed opportunities, whether in your career, education, or personal life. When you take action, you avoid missing out on chances to learn, grow, and achieve your goals. This can lead to long-term regrets and dissatisfaction with your life and achievements. Overcoming procrastination is essential to seizing opportunities and maximizing your chances.

4. **Compromised Quality of Work**: Procrastination often forces you to rush through tasks at the last minute, leading to compromised quality of work. When you don't give yourself enough time to do a task properly, you're more likely to make mistakes, overlook important details, and produce subpar results. This can damage your reputation, whether professionally or personally, leading to further negative consequences.

5. **Impact on Relationships**: Procrastination can also strain personal and professional relationships. When you consistently fail to meet deadlines or fulfill commitments, others may perceive you as unreliable or disorganized. This can lead to a breakdown in trust and respect, which can harm your relationships and limit your opportunities for collaboration and support.

Overcoming procrastination requires a combination of self-awareness, practical strategies, and a commitment to change. Here are some effective strategies for addressing procrastination and fostering a more disciplined approach to your goals:

1. **Break Tasks into Smaller Steps**: One of the most effective ways to overcome procrastination is to break large tasks into smaller, more manageable steps. This reduces the feeling of overwhelm and makes it easier to get started. For example, if you need to write a report, break the task down into steps such as researching, creating an outline, writing the introduction, etc. Focusing on a tiny step at a time can build momentum and make consistent progress.

2. **Set Specific Deadlines**: Setting specific deadlines for each task or step can help create a sense of urgency and

accountability. Instead of having a vague deadline like "sometime next week," set a specific date and time by which the task must be completed. This helps prevent procrastination by giving you a clear target to aim for. Share your deadlines with someone else to create external accountability.

3. **Use the Pomodoro Technique**: The Pomodoro Technique is a time management method that can help you stay focused and overcome procrastination. It involves working in short, concentrated intervals (typically 25 minutes) followed by a short break (5 minutes). After four intervals, take a longer break (15-30 minutes). This technique helps you break tasks into manageable chunks, reduces the temptation to procrastinate, and makes staying focused on the task at hand easier.

4. **Eliminate Distractions**: Distractions are one of the most significant contributors to procrastination. To overcome procrastination, identify and eliminate distractions in your environment. This might involve turning off notifications on your phone, blocking distracting websites, or creating a dedicated workspace free from interruptions. By minimizing distractions, you create an environment that supports focus and productivity.

5. **Practice Self-Compassion**: Self-compassion is an essential tool for overcoming procrastination; instead of criticizing yourself for procrastinating, practice self-compassion by acknowledging your challenges and treating yourself with kindness. Recognize that procrastination is a common struggle and doesn't define your worth or abilities. By practicing self-compassion, you can reduce the negative

emotions that often fuel procrastination and create a more positive mindset for taking action.

6. **Visualize the Benefits of Taking Action**: Visualization can be a powerful motivator for overcoming procrastination. Take a few moments to visualize the benefits of completing the task you're avoiding. Imagine how you will feel once the task is done, the sense of accomplishment you will experience, and its positive impact on your goals. By focusing on the benefits of taking action, you can shift your mindset from avoidance to motivation.

7. **Apply the Two-Minute Rule**: The two-minute rule is a simple but effective strategy for overcoming procrastination. The idea is that if a task takes less than two minutes to complete, do it immediately. This helps prevent small tasks from piling up and becoming overwhelming. Additionally, the two-minute rule can overcome resistance to starting larger tasks. Committing to just two minutes of work makes it easier to continue once you've started.

8. **Reward Yourself for Taking Action**: Positive reinforcement can be a powerful motivator for overcoming procrastination. Create a system of rewards for yourself when you complete tasks, especially those you've been avoiding. The reward doesn't have to be significant; it could be something as simple as taking a short break, enjoying a treat, or doing something you enjoy. By associating positive outcomes with taking action, you can reduce the appeal of procrastination and increase your motivation to get things done.

9. **Reflect on Your Procrastination Triggers**: To effectively overcome procrastination, it's essential to reflect on the specific triggers that lead you to delay tasks—attention to the

thoughts, emotions, and circumstances contributing to procrastination. Once you've identified these triggers, you can develop strategies to address them, such as reframing negative thoughts, managing stress, or adjusting your environment. Understanding your procrastination triggers can help you take proactive steps to prevent procrastination in the future.

10. **Seek Support and Accountability**: Sometimes, overcoming procrastination is easier with the support of others. Share your goals and deadlines with a trusted friend, mentor, or coach who can provide encouragement and hold you accountable. Regular check-ins with someone who supports your efforts can help you stay on track and make progress, even when you feel tempted to procrastinate.

CONCLUSION: TAKING CONTROL OF PROCRASTINATION

Procrastination is a common but conquerable challenge on the path to success. By understanding the root causes of procrastination and implementing practical strategies, you can control your time and energy and stay disciplined and focused on your goals. Overcoming procrastination is not eliminating it but developing the tools and habits to manage it effectively. With consistent effort and a commitment to change, you can break free from the cycle of procrastination and build the discipline needed to achieve lasting success.

The next chapter will explore managing distractions and staying focused, another critical aspect of maintaining discipline and achieving your goals. By learning to minimize distractions and enhance your concentration, you can create an environment that supports your best work and helps you stay on track.

6

MANAGING DISTRACTIONS AND STAYING FOCUSED

In today's fast-paced, hyper-connected world, distractions are everywhere. From the constant buzz of notifications on our smartphones to the lure of social media and endless online content streams, staying focused on our goals can be a significant challenge. Yet, managing distractions and maintaining focus are essential skills for achieving success and maintaining discipline. In this chapter, we will explore the impact of distractions on productivity and discipline, identify familiar sources of distraction, and provide practical strategies for minimizing distractions and enhancing focus.

Distractions can profoundly impact productivity and self-discipline. Every time we are interrupted or distracted, our attention is pulled away from the task at hand, making it more challenging to complete it efficiently and effectively. Research shows that it can take an average of 23 minutes to regain focus after being distracted, which means that even brief interruptions can significantly reduce productivity.

When distractions are frequent and unmanaged, they can reduce self-discipline, making it harder to stay on track toward long-term goals. The constant switching between tasks, known as "task-switching," reduces work quality and increases cognitive fatigue. This mental exhaustion can lead to procrastination, mistakes, and a decline in overall performance. Moreover, the more we allow distractions to take over our time and attention, the more we reinforce the habit of giving in to them, making it even more challenging to develop and maintain focus in the future.

Distractions also affect our ability to achieve a state of "flow," a mental state where we are fully immersed and engaged in a task. Flow is often associated with peak performance and creativity but requires sustained concentration and minimal interruptions. When distractions constantly pull us out of flow, we miss out on the opportunity to perform at our best and experience the satisfaction that comes from deep, focused work.

COMMON SOURCES OF DISTRACTION

To effectively manage distractions, it's essential to identify the most common sources of distraction in your life. These can vary from person to person, but some of the most prevalent distractions include:

1. **Digital Devices**: Smartphones, tablets, and computers are among the most common sources of distraction. Notifications from social media, emails, text messages, and apps constantly compete for our attention. Even when we're not actively using these devices, the mere presence of a smartphone can reduce cognitive capacity and focus.

2. **Social Media**: Social media platforms are designed to be highly engaging, often leading to hours of mindless scrolling. The instant gratification and endless content make it easy to lose track of time and divert attention away from more critical tasks.

3. **Multitasking**: Many people believe that multitasking is an effective way to get more done, but research shows that it reduces productivity and increases the likelihood of errors. Switching between tasks disrupts focus and makes it difficult to complete any single task effectively.

4. **External Interruptions**: Interruptions from coworkers, family members, or environmental noise can break concentration and disrupt workflow. Even brief interruptions can disrupt focus and make it challenging to regain momentum.

5. **Internal Distractions**: Internal distractions, such as daydreaming, stress, or worrying about unrelated tasks, can also pull attention away from the task. Because they originate from within, these distractions are often more complicated to manage.

6. **Environmental Factors**: Your physical environment can either support or hinder your ability to focus. A cluttered workspace, uncomfortable seating, or poor lighting can create distractions that make concentrating difficult.

PRACTICAL STRATEGIES FOR MINIMIZING DISTRACTIONS

While distractions are a natural part of life, there are several strategies you can implement to minimize them and improve your ability to focus. Creating an environment that supports concentration and developing habits that promote sustained attention can enhance your productivity and maintain the discipline needed to achieve your goals.

1. **Create a Dedicated Workspace**: Your workspace can signal your brain that it's time to focus. Choose a quiet, comfortable location free from distractions and set it up to support your work. Keep your workspace organized and clutter-free; a tidy environment can help reduce mental distractions. If possible, separate your workspace from areas associated with leisure or relaxation, such as your bed or living room, to create a clear boundary between work and rest.

2. **Limit Digital Distractions**: Managing digital distractions is essential for maintaining focus. Start by turning off non-essential notifications on your phone, computer, and other devices. Consider using "Do Not Disturb" mode during focused work or use apps and tools that block distracting websites and apps during designated times. Consider setting specific times for checking emails and social media rather than allowing them to interrupt your workflow throughout the day.

3. **Practice time Blocking**: Time blocking is a time management technique where you schedule specific blocks of time for focused work on particular tasks. By dedicating uninterrupted time to each task, you can reduce the temptation to multitask and minimize distractions. During these blocks, focus solely on the task and avoid switching between tasks. Time blocking helps you stay organized and creates a sense of urgency that can boost productivity.

4. **Use the Pomodoro Technique**: The Pomodoro Technique is another effective method for managing distractions and maintaining focus. This technique involves working in short, focused intervals (typically 25 minutes) followed by a brief break (5 minutes). After four intervals, take a longer break (15-30 minutes). The structured breaks help prevent burnout and keep your mind fresh, while the timed intervals create a sense of discipline and accountability.

5. **Minimize External Interruptions**: To reduce external interruptions, communicate your need for focused work time to those around you. If you work in a shared space, consider using visual cues, such as headphones or a "Do Not Disturb" sign, to indicate that you're not to be interrupted. If noise is a distraction, use noise-canceling headphones or listen to background music that helps you concentrate. Additionally, schedule meetings, calls, and other interruptions during specific times of the day so they don't interfere with your most productive hours.

6. **Practice Mindfulness and Meditation**: Mindfulness and meditation can help you manage internal distractions and

stay focused. By practicing mindfulness, you learn to become more aware of your thoughts and emotions without getting carried away. This awareness lets you recognize your mind wandering and gently redirect your focus to the task. Regular meditation practice can strengthen your ability to concentrate, reduce stress, and enhance overall mental clarity.

7. **Set Clear Goals and Priorities**: Setting clear goals and priorities can help you focus on what matters most. At the start of each day, identify the most critical tasks that you need to accomplish and prioritize them. Concentrating on your top priorities first ensures you're progressing on the functions with the most significant impact. Having clear goals also makes it easier to say no to distractions and less important tasks that don't align with your objectives.

8. **Take Regular Breaks**: While it may seem counterintuitive, regular breaks are essential for maintaining focus and preventing burnout. Breaks give your brain a chance to rest and recharge, which can improve your ability to concentrate when you return to work. Use your breaks to step away from your workspace, stretch, move around, or do something enjoyable that helps you relax. Short breaks throughout the day can boost productivity and help you stay focused over the long term.

9. **Manage Stress and Mental Clutter**: Stress and mental clutter can be significant internal distractions that hinder focus. To manage stress, practice relaxation techniques such as deep breathing, yoga, or progressive muscle relaxation. Additionally, consider using a journal to clear your mind by writing down thoughts, worries, or ideas

that may distract you. Addressing mental clutter creates more mental space to focus on your tasks.

10. **Reflect and Adjust**: Regularly reflect on your work habits and adjust as needed. Pay attention to the sources of distraction in your life and evaluate which strategies are most effective in minimizing them. By being mindful of how you manage your time and attention, you can continuously improve your ability to stay focused and disciplined.

BUILDING A FOCUSED MINDSET

Beyond external strategies, cultivating a focused mindset is essential for long-term success in managing distractions. A concentrated mindset involves prioritizing what matters most and resisting the urge to be constantly busy or multitasking. It requires a deep understanding of your goals and values and the discipline to align your actions.

1. **Embrace Single-Tasking**: Instead of trying to do multiple things at once, practice single-tasking—focusing on one task until it's complete. Single-tasking allows you to give your full attention to the task at hand, which can improve the quality of your work and reduce the likelihood of mistakes. It also helps to create a sense of flow and deep engagement, making the job more satisfying and enjoyable.

2. **Prioritize Deep Work**: Author Cal Newport popularized the concept of focused, undistracted work that allows you to produce your best results. Prioritize deep work by setting aside dedicated time each day for tasks that require intense concentration and creativity. Protect this time from interruptions and distractions and treat it as sacred. Regularly engaging in deep work can significantly progress your most important goals.

3. **Practice Patience and Persistence**: Developing a focused mindset takes time and persistence. Be patient with yourself as you build new habits and learn to manage distractions more effectively. Recognize that focus is a skill that can be improved with practice and celebrate small victories along the way. Over time, your ability to stay focused will become more robust, and you'll be better equipped to handle the challenges and distractions that come your way.

CONCLUSION: THE POWER OF FOCUS IN ACHIEVING SUCCESS

Managing distractions and staying focused are essential components of self-discipline and success. In a world filled with endless distractions, the ability to concentrate on what truly matters is a rare and valuable skill. By implementing practical strategies to minimize distractions, cultivating a focused mindset, and prioritizing deep work, you can enhance productivity, maintain discipline, and achieve your goals more effectively.

In the next chapter, we will explore developing mental toughness, a critical attribute that helps you stay disciplined and resilient in facing challenges. By building mental toughness, you can navigate setbacks, maintain focus, and continue progressing toward your long-term goals.

DEVELOPING MENTAL TOUGHNESS

Mental toughness is a crucial quality that enables individuals to stay disciplined, resilient and focused in the face of challenges and adversity. The inner strength allows you to keep pushing forward when circumstances are complicated, and the temptation to quit is strong. Developing mental toughness is not just about enduring hardships; it's about thriving in the midst of them and using challenges as stepping stones toward tremendous success. In this chapter, we will explore the concept of mental toughness, discuss its importance, and provide practical strategies to cultivate it.

Mental toughness is often described as the ability to persevere and remain focused in the face of stress, pressure, and setbacks. It's what separates those who achieve their goals from those who give up when the going gets tough. Mental toughness is not a fixed trait you either have or don't have; it's a skill that can be developed and strengthened over time through intentional practice and effort.

At its core, mental toughness involves several key components:

1. **Resilience**: Resilience is the ability to bounce back from setbacks and keep moving forward, even when things don't go as planned. It's about viewing failures and obstacles as opportunities to learn and grow rather than as reasons to give up. Resilient individuals can maintain a positive outlook and stay committed to their goals, even in adversity.

2. **Confidence**: Confidence is a crucial aspect of mental toughness. It's the belief in overcoming challenges and achieving your goals. Mentally tough individuals have a strong sense of self-belief, allowing them to stay focused and motivated, even when others doubt them or face difficult circumstances.

3. **Focus**: Mental toughness requires maintaining focus on one's goals, even when distractions or obstacles arise. This means staying disciplined and avoiding getting sidetracked by short-term temptations or setbacks. Mentally tough individuals can keep their eyes on the prize and continue working toward their goals, no matter their challenges.

4. **Emotional Regulation**: Effective emotion management is a critical component of mental toughness. It involves staying calm and composed under pressure and not letting

emotions like fear, anger, or frustration disrupt progress. Mentally tough individuals can maintain emotional balance, which allows them to think clearly and make rational decisions, even in stressful situations.

5. **Commitment**: Mental toughness also involves a deep commitment to your goals and values. It's about having a strong sense of purpose and being willing to put in the effort required to achieve your objectives. This commitment drives you to keep going, even when the journey is complex, and the rewards are not immediately visible.

THE IMPORTANCE OF MENTAL TOUGHNESS

Mental toughness is essential for achieving long-term success in any area of life. Whether you're pursuing a career goal, working on personal development, or striving to improve your health and fitness, mental toughness is what allows you to stay the course and overcome the inevitable challenges that arise along the way.

1. **Overcoming Adversity**: Life is full of challenges, and how you respond to them can determine your success or failure. Mental toughness enables you to face adversity head-on and turn obstacles into opportunities for growth; rather than being discouraged by setbacks, mentally tough individuals use them to push harder and reach new levels of achievement.

2. **Sustaining Long-Term Effort**: Many goals require sustained effort over a long period. Mental toughness helps you maintain the discipline and motivation needed to keep working toward your goals, even when progress is slow, or you encounter difficulties. It lets you stay consistent and persistent, even when the initial excitement has worn off.

3. **Handling Pressure**: Pressure is an unavoidable part of life, whether in a high-stakes job, competitive sports, or personal relationships. Mental toughness helps you stay calm and composed under pressure, allowing you to perform at your best when it matters most. It also lets you maintain your confidence and focus, even in the face of criticism or high expectations.

4. **Achieving Personal Growth**: Mental toughness is closely linked to personal growth and self-improvement. When you're mentally tough, you're more likely to take on challenges, step out of your comfort zone, and push yourself to achieve your full potential. This willingness to embrace discomfort and face difficult situations leads to more significant personal and professional development.

5. **Building Resilient Relationships**: Mental toughness also plays a role in building strong, resilient relationships. Whether in your personal life or professional life, relationships often require patience, understanding, and the ability to navigate conflicts and challenges. Mentally tough individuals are better equipped to handle these situations gracefully and maintain positive, healthy relationships.

Developing mental toughness is a gradual process that involves building resilience, strengthening your mindset, and cultivating habits that support your long-term goals. Here are several strategies to help you develop and enhance your mental toughness:

1. **Embrace Challenges**: One of the most effective ways to build mental toughness is to challenge yourself and step out of your comfort zone regularly. This could involve taking on new responsibilities at work, pursuing a problematic personal goal, or facing fear head-on. By consistently pushing yourself to tackle challenges, you build the confidence and resilience needed to handle adversity in the future.

2. **Cultivate a Growth Mindset**: A growth mindset is the belief that your abilities and intelligence can be developed through effort and learning. This mindset is critical to mental toughness because it encourages you to see challenges as growth opportunities rather than threats to your self-worth. To cultivate a growth mindset, focus on the process of learning and improvement rather than on the outcome. Embrace mistakes as learning opportunities, and view setbacks as part of the journey toward success.

3. **Practice Emotional Regulation**: Learning to manage your emotions is essential for developing mental toughness. This involves recognizing your feelings, understanding their triggers, and developing strategies to manage them effectively. Techniques such as mindfulness, meditation, and deep breathing can help you stay calm and centered in stressful situations. Practicing gratitude and positive

self-talk can help you maintain a positive outlook and build emotional resilience.

4. **Set Clear, Meaningful Goals**: Mental toughness is closely linked to having a clear sense of purpose and direction. Setting meaningful goals that align with your values and passions provides the motivation and drive needed to stay disciplined and focused. Break your goals down into smaller, manageable steps, and celebrate your progress along the way. This will help you stay committed and maintain your mental toughness, even when the journey is challenging.

5. **Develop a Routine**: Establishing a daily routine supporting your goals can help you build mental toughness by creating structure and consistency. A routine provides a sense of control and predictability, which can help you stay focused and disciplined. Include habits that promote physical, mental, and emotional well-being, such as regular exercise, healthy eating, and time for reflection or meditation.

6. **Learn from Setbacks**: Setbacks are inevitable, but they don't have to disrupt your progress. Mentally tough individuals view setbacks as opportunities to learn and grow. When you encounter a setback, take the time to reflect on what went wrong, what you can learn from the experience, and how you can improve in the future. This proactive approach helps you develop resilience and prepares you to handle future challenges more confidently.

7. **Surround Yourself with Positive Influences**: The people you surround yourself with can significantly impact your

mental toughness. Seek out relationships with individuals who inspire, challenge, and support you. Surround yourself with positive influences that encourage you to stay focused on your goals and help you navigate difficult situations. Avoid toxic relationships that drain your energy and undermine your confidence.

8. **Practice Self-Compassion**: Developing mental toughness doesn't mean being hard on yourself or ignoring your emotions. Self-compassion is a critical component of mental toughness. It involves treating yourself with kindness and understanding, especially in moments of failure or difficulty. By being gentle with yourself, you can recover more quickly from setbacks and maintain your motivation and focus.

9. **Visualize Success**: Visualization is a powerful tool for building mental toughness. Regularly visualizing yourself achieving your goals and overcoming challenges can build confidence and reinforce your commitment to your objectives. Visualize the successful outcome, the steps to get there, and how you will handle potential obstacles.

10. **Stay Committed to Your Values**: Mental toughness is rooted in a strong sense of purpose and values. Stay connected to your core values and use them to guide your decisions and actions. When you're clear about what matters most, it becomes easier to stay disciplined and focused, even when faced with challenges or temptations.

Developing mental toughness is an ongoing journey that requires patience, persistence, and practice. It's about building the resilience, confidence, and focus needed to stay disciplined and achieve your goals, even in adversity. By embracing challenges, cultivating a growth mindset, and practicing emotional regulation, you can strengthen your mental toughness and unlock your full potential.

The next chapter will explore the relationship between time management and discipline. Effective time management is essential for maintaining focus, avoiding procrastination, and achieving long-term success. By mastering time management skills, you can maximize your time and stay on track toward your goals.

8

TIME MANAGEMENT AND PRIORITIZATION

Time is one of our most valuable resources, yet it is also one of the most difficult to manage effectively. Good time management and prioritization are essential for maintaining discipline, achieving goals, and finding balance. When we manage our time well, we can focus on what truly matters, avoid unnecessary stress, and create a sense of control over our daily lives. This chapter will explore the importance of time management, discuss various time management techniques, and provide strategies for effective prioritization.

Effective time management is crucial for several reasons. First and foremost, it allows us to make the most of our limited time each day. Whether working on a career goal, pursuing personal development, or balancing multiple responsibilities, managing your time effectively ensures you use your hours wisely.

1. **Increased Productivity**: When you manage your time well, you can accomplish more in less time. This increased productivity comes from focusing on the most critical tasks and avoiding wasting time on unproductive activities. Time management helps you stay organized, minimize distractions, and work more efficiently, allowing you to achieve your goals faster.

2. **Reduced Stress**: Poor time management often leads to stress, as you may find yourself rushing to meet deadlines, juggling multiple tasks, or feeling overwhelmed by a long to-do list. By managing your time effectively, you can reduce this stress by creating a clear plan for your day, setting realistic deadlines, and giving yourself enough time to complete tasks without feeling pressured.

3. **Better Work-Life Balance**: Time management is essential for maintaining a healthy work-life balance. When you prioritize your time effectively, you can ensure that you're dedicating enough time to both work and personal life, preventing burnout and ensuring that you have time for rest, relaxation, and activities that bring you joy.

4. **Improved Decision-Making**: Effective time management also enhances decision-making. When you have a clear plan and prioritize your tasks, you can make decisions more

quickly and confidently, knowing you're focusing on what truly matters. This reduces the mental clutter that can arise from trying to do too much at once and allows you to think more clearly and strategically.

5. **Achieving Long-Term Goals**: Many long-term goals require consistent effort over time. Effective time management helps you break down these goals into smaller, manageable tasks and ensures that you're making steady progress toward your objectives. By managing your time well, you can stay on track with your goals and avoid the frustration of feeling like you need to make progress.

TIME MANAGEMENT TECHNIQUES

Several time management techniques can help you make the most of your time and stay focused on your goals. By experimenting with different methods, you can find your best approach.

1. **The Eisenhower Matrix**: The Eisenhower Matrix, also known as the Urgent-Important Matrix, is a simple yet powerful tool for prioritizing tasks. The matrix divides tasks into four categories based on their urgency and importance:

   o **Urgent and Important**: Your top priority should be urgent and important tasks. These tasks often have immediate deadlines and significant consequences if not completed. Examples include critical work projects, emergencies, and pressing deadlines.

   o **Important but Not Urgent**: These tasks are important for long-term goals but don't require immediate attention. They often include activities like planning, skill development, and relationship building. Prioritize these tasks after completing urgent and important tasks.

o **Urgent but Not Important**: Tasks in this category may seem urgent but contribute little to your long-term goals. They can often be delegated or scheduled for later. Examples include some meetings, interruptions, and minor tasks.

o **Not Urgent and Not Important**: These tasks are neither urgent nor important and should be minimized or eliminated. They often include distractions like excessive social media use, unnecessary emails, and time-wasting activities.

By categorizing your tasks using the Eisenhower Matrix, you can focus on what truly matters and avoid getting caught up in less important activities.

2. **Time Blocking**: Time blocking involves scheduling specific blocks for daily tasks or activities. Instead of working from a to-do list, you assign each task a particular time slot on your calendar. This technique helps you focus on one task at a time, reducing the multitasking temptation. It also ensures that you're dedicating enough time to essential tasks and prevents you from spending too much time on less critical activities.

To implement time blocking, start by identifying your most important tasks for the day and assigning them time slots. Be realistic about each task's length and build in buffer time for unexpected interruptions or delays. Stick to your schedule as closely as possible and adjust to accommodate changes.

3. **The Pomodoro Technique**: As referenced in the previous chapters, the Pomodoro Technique is a time management method that involves working in short, focused intervals (usually 25 minutes) followed by a short break (5 minutes). After four intervals, take a longer break (15-30 minutes). This technique helps you maintain focus and productivity by breaking your work into manageable chunks and providing regular opportunities for rest.

To use the Pomodoro Technique, start by choosing a task to work on and set a timer for 25 minutes. Work on the task until the timer goes off, then take a 5-minute break. Repeat this process and take a more extended break after four intervals. This method can help you stay motivated and avoid burnout, especially during long work sessions.

4. **The Two-Minute Rule**: The Two-Minute Rule is a simple yet effective strategy for managing small tasks as mentioned in chapter five. It states that if a task takes less than two minutes to complete, do it immediately. This helps prevent small tasks from piling up and becoming overwhelming. The Two-Minute Rule is applicable for managing quick functions like responding to emails, making a phone call, or tidying up your workspace.

By dealing with these small tasks right away, you can manage your to-do list and free up mental space for more important activities.

5. **The 80/20 Rule (Pareto Principle)**: The 80/20 Rule, also known as the Pareto Principle, states that 80% of your results come from 20% of your efforts. In other words, a small portion of your tasks or activities are responsible for most of your success. To apply this principle to time management, focus on identifying and prioritizing the 20%

of tasks that significantly impact your goals. Concentrating on these high-impact activities can help you achieve more with less effort and time.

6. **Batching Similar Tasks**: Task batching involves grouping and completing similar tasks in one session. For example, batch functions like answering emails, making phone calls, or running errands. This approach reduces the cognitive load associated with switching between different types of tasks and helps you work more efficiently.

To implement task batching, review your to-do list and identify tasks that can be grouped. Schedule a specific time to complete these tasks in one session rather than spreading them throughout the day.

7. **Prioritization by Energy Levels**: Your energy levels fluctuate throughout the day, and different tasks require different energy and focus levels. To maximize productivity, align your most important and demanding tasks with your peak energy levels. For example, schedule your most important work if you're most alert and focused in the morning. Save less critical or routine tasks for times when your energy is lower.

By matching your tasks to your energy levels, you can work more effectively and avoid burnout.

EFFECTIVE PRIORITIZATION

Prioritization is a crucial aspect of time management. It involves determining which tasks are most important and focusing your efforts on completing them first. Effective prioritization ensures that you're making progress on your most important goals, even when your time is limited.

1. **Align Tasks with Long-Term Goals**: When prioritizing your tasks, consider how each contributes to your long-term goals. Focus on activities that directly impact your success and avoid getting caught up in tasks that don't align with your objectives. This may require saying no to less critical tasks or delegating them to others.

To align your tasks with your long-term goals, regularly review your goals and evaluate your to-do list considering these objectives. Prioritize tasks that move you closer to your goals and deprioritize or eliminate tasks that don't.

2. **Use the ABCDE Method**: The ABCDE Method is a prioritization technique that involves categorizing tasks based on their importance:

   o **A Tasks**: These are essential tasks that must be done. Completing them will have significant positive consequences while failing will have serious negative consequences.

   o **B Tasks**: These are important but less critical than A tasks. They should be completed, but the consequences of not achieving them are less severe.

   o **C Tasks** are pleasant tasks with little to no impact on your long-term goals. They can be done if time permits but should not be prioritized over A and B tasks.

   o **D Tasks**: These are tasks that can be delegated to others. If possible, delegate these tasks to free up your time for more critical activities.

- ○ **E Tasks**: These are tasks that can be eliminated. If a task doesn't contribute to your goals and isn't necessary, consider removing it from your to-do list.

By categorizing your tasks using the ABCDE Method, you can ensure that you focus on the most critical activities and make the best use of your time.

3. **Review and Adjust**: Prioritization is not a one-time activity; it requires regular review and adjustment. As new tasks and responsibilities arise, re-evaluate your priorities and adjust your plan. This flexibility ensures you focus on what matters most, even when circumstances change.

To review your priorities, schedule time each week to assess your progress and plan for the upcoming week. Reflect on what went well, what didn't, and how you can adjust your priorities to stay on track with your goals.

4. **Avoid Perfectionism**: Perfectionism can be a significant barrier to effective prioritization. When you strive for perfection, you may spend too much time on tasks that don't require it, leading to inefficiency and burnout. To overcome perfectionism, focus on completing tasks to a high standard without getting bogged down in unnecessary details. Recognize that it's better to complete a task well and on time than to delay it in pursuit of perfection.

5. **Delegate When Possible**: Delegation is an essential skill for effective prioritization. If you have tasks others can do, delegate them to free up your time for more critical activities. Delegation allows you to focus on high-priority tasks and empowers others to take on responsibility and develop their skills.

To delegate effectively, identify tasks that don't require your specific expertise and assign them to someone who can complete them. Provide clear instructions and support as needed but trust the person to handle the task independently.

CONCLUSION: MASTERING TIME MANAGEMENT AND PRIORITIZATION

Time management and prioritization are essential skills for achieving success and maintaining discipline. By managing your time effectively and prioritizing tasks that align with your goals, you can make the most of each day, reduce stress, and achieve a better work-life balance. The techniques and strategies discussed in this chapter provide a foundation for managing time wisely and staying focused on what truly matters.

The next chapter will explore the importance of sustaining discipline over the long term. While it's one thing to develop discipline, maintaining it consistently over time requires ongoing effort, reflection, and adjustment. By understanding the challenges and strategies for sustaining discipline, you can continue progressing toward your goals and achieve lasting success.

9

SUSTAINING DISCIPLINE OVER THE LONG-TERM

Discipline is the backbone of success but sustaining it over the long term can be one of the most challenging aspects of personal and professional growth. It's not enough to develop discipline for a short period; true success requires maintaining consistent effort and focus over weeks, months, or even years. In this chapter, we will explore the importance of long-term discipline, the common challenges in sustaining it, and practical strategies to help you maintain your discipline over time.

Discipline is more than just the ability to work hard or stay focused for a short Time. It's about the sustained commitment to your goals, values, and the processes that lead to success. Whether working on improving your health, advancing your career, or developing a new skill, the results you seek are often the product of consistent, long-term effort.

1. **Achieving Long-Term Goals**: Many of life's most significant and rewarding achievements require sustained effort over a long period. For instance, earning a degree, building a successful business, or achieving a fitness goal are all long-term endeavors that cannot be accomplished overnight. Sustaining discipline is essential to ensure that you continue progressing toward these goals, even when faced with obstacles or when the initial excitement has worn off.

2. **Building Resilience**: Long-term discipline helps build resilience, the ability to bounce back from setbacks and continue pursuing your goals. Resilience is developed through the experience of overcoming challenges and persisting in the face of difficulties. By sustaining discipline, you strengthen your ability to handle adversity, making it easier to stay committed to your goals in the future.

3. **Consistency Leads to Mastery**: Consistency is critical to mastery, whether learning a new skill or improving an existing one—repeated practice and effort over time lead to incremental improvements, which accumulate and result in significant progress. Sustaining discipline ensures that you continue to put in the necessary work, allowing you to achieve a level of expertise that would be impossible with intermittent or short-lived efforts.

4. **Maintaining Momentum**: Discipline creates momentum, the forward motion that helps you keep going even when motivation decreases. Once you establish a routine or habit, it becomes easier to maintain that momentum, as the effort required to continue is less than the effort needed to start again after a break. Sustaining discipline allows you to build on your successes and maintain your progress rather than losing ground and starting over.

5. **Long-Term Fulfillment**: Over the long term, sustaining discipline contributes to a more profound sense of fulfillment and satisfaction. When you commit to a goal and see it through to completion, you experience a sense of accomplishment far more rewarding than short-term gratification. This long-term fulfillment results from knowing you've done the work and achieved something meaningful.

COMMON CHALLENGES IN SUSTAINING DISCIPLINE

While the benefits of long-term discipline are clear, sustaining it can be challenging. Several common obstacles can undermine your efforts to maintain discipline over time.

1. **Burnout**: One of the most significant challenges in sustaining discipline is burnout. Burnout occurs when prolonged stress, overwork, or a lack of balance leads to physical, emotional, and mental exhaustion. When you're burned out, it becomes difficult to maintain the energy and motivation needed to stay disciplined. Burnout often results from pushing too hard for too long without taking adequate breaks or allowing time for recovery.

2. **Loss of Motivation**: Motivation is often high at the beginning of a new endeavor but can decrease over time, especially when slow progress or obstacles arise. When motivation decreases, it becomes harder to maintain the discipline required to keep going. This loss of motivation can be particularly challenging when the rewards of your efforts are only sometimes visible.

3. **Plateaus and Setbacks**: During any long-term pursuit, there will be periods where progress slows or stops altogether. These plateaus can be frustrating and can lead to a loss of confidence and discipline. Setbacks, such as unexpected challenges or failures, can also shake your resolve and make it difficult to stay committed to your goals.

4. **Distractions and Temptations**: It's easy to lose focus on your long-term goals in a world full of distractions. Whether it's the lure of instant gratification, the demands of daily life, or the influence of others, distractions can pull you away from the disciplined actions required to achieve your goals. Over time, these distractions can reduce your discipline and lead to losing momentum.

5. **Complacency**: Once you've made some progress toward your goals, it's easy to become complacent and start to relax your efforts. Complacency can lead to a decline in discipline, as you may begin to feel that you've already achieved enough or can afford to take it easy. However, this mindset can stall your progress and prevent you from reaching your full potential.

While the challenges of sustaining discipline are real, there are several strategies you can use to overcome them and maintain your commitment over time.

1. **Set Realistic and Flexible Goals**: Setting realistic goals is essential for sustaining discipline. You may quickly become overwhelmed or discouraged if your goals are too ambitious or unrealistic. Instead, break your long-term goals into smaller, manageable milestones that you can achieve step by step. Additionally, be flexible in your approach. Life is unpredictable, and circumstances may change, so adjusting your goals and plans as needed while keeping your eyes on the bigger picture is essential.

2. **Incorporate Rest and Recovery**: To avoid burnout, it's crucial to incorporate regular rest and recovery into your routine. This means taking breaks, getting enough sleep, and allowing yourself time to recharge. Rest is not a sign of weakness or lack of discipline; it's necessary to maintain long-term productivity and well-being. By prioritizing rest, you ensure you have the energy and focus needed to sustain your efforts.

3. **Revisit Your "Why"**: When motivation decreases, it's helpful to revisit the reasons behind your goals. Why did you set these goals in the first place? What do you hope to achieve or experience due to your efforts? By reconnecting with your deeper motivations and values, you can reignite your commitment and find the strength to keep going, even when the going gets tough. Keeping a journal or vision board can help you regularly remind yourself of your "why."

4. **Celebrate Progress, Not Perfection**: It's essential to recognize and celebrate your progress, even if it's not perfect. Perfectionism can lead to frustration and burnout, so focus on incremental improvements and successes. Celebrate small wins and milestones and use them as motivation to keep moving forward. Acknowledging your progress builds momentum and reinforces the positive habits that lead to sustained discipline.

5. **Stay Accountable**: Accountability is a powerful tool for sustaining discipline. Whether through a coach, mentor, accountability partner, or support group, having someone to check in with can help you stay on track. Accountability provides external motivation, encouragement, and a sense of responsibility to others. It also lets you stay honest about your progress and challenges.

6. **Embrace the Process**: Sustaining discipline is not just about the result; it's about embracing growth and improvement. Rather than focusing solely on the outcome, learn to enjoy the journey and the small steps you take each day. By finding satisfaction in the process, you can stay motivated and disciplined, even when progress is slow, or the goal seems distant.

7. **Adapt to Challenges**: Challenges and setbacks are inevitable in any long-term pursuit, but they don't have to disrupt your discipline. Instead, view challenges as opportunities to learn and grow. When you encounter obstacles, take a step back, assess the situation, and adapt your approach. Flexibility and resilience are vital components of sustained discipline, allowing you to navigate difficulties without losing sight of your goals.

8. **Create Rituals and Routines**: Establishing rituals and routines can help reinforce discipline by creating structure and consistency in your daily life. These routines can serve as anchors that keep you grounded and focused, even when external circumstances change. Whether it's a morning routine setting the day's tone or a nightly ritual that helps you wind down and reflect, these habits provide a sense of stability and purpose.

9. **Focus on What You Can Control**: In any long-term endeavor, there will be factors beyond your control. Rather than getting discouraged by these external forces, focus on what you can control: your actions, attitudes, and responses. By directing your energy toward the things you can influence, you maintain a sense of agency and empowerment, essential for sustaining discipline.

10. **Reflect and Adjust Regularly**: Sustaining discipline requires ongoing reflection and adjustment. Set aside time regularly to evaluate your progress, consider what's working and what's not, and make any necessary changes to your approach. This practice of continuous improvement helps you stay aligned with your goals and ensures that you're making the most of your efforts.

CONCLUSION: THE PATH TO LASTING SUCCESS

Sustaining discipline over the long term is essential for achieving meaningful, lasting success. While the journey may be challenging, the rewards of consistent effort, resilience, and perseverance are well worth it. By setting realistic goals, incorporating rest and recovery, staying accountable, and embracing the process, you can maintain the discipline needed to reach your full potential.

In the final chapter, we will explore the importance of creating a personal discipline plan—a roadmap that integrates the concepts and strategies discussed throughout this book. This plan will guide you in maintaining discipline and achieving your long-term goals, ensuring you have the tools and techniques needed for continued success.

10

CREATING A PERSONAL DISCIPLINE PLAN

Throughout this book, we've explored the various facets of discipline, from understanding its importance to managing distractions, building habits, overcoming procrastination, and sustaining long-term effort. It's time to combine all these elements into a cohesive personal discipline plan—a roadmap guiding you toward achieving your goals and maintaining the discipline necessary for long-term success.

A personal discipline plan is a customized strategy for staying focused, organized, and motivated. It's not a one-size-fits-all approach; it's tailored to your unique goals, strengths, and challenges. In this chapter, we'll discuss the critical components of a personal discipline plan and provide step-by-step guidance on creating one that works for you.

The primary purpose of a personal discipline plan is to provide structure and direction for your efforts. Without a plan, it's easy to become overwhelmed by the demands of daily life, maintain sight of your long-term goals, or fall into patterns of procrastination and distraction. A well-crafted discipline plan helps you stay on track by breaking down your goals into actionable steps, identifying potential obstacles, and outlining strategies for overcoming them.

1. **Clarity and Focus**: A personal discipline plan clarifies your goals and priorities, helping you focus on what truly matters. By defining your objectives and the steps needed to achieve them, you create a clear path forward, reducing uncertainty and confusion.

2. **Accountability**: Your discipline plan serves as a tool for accountability. It provides a reference point for tracking your progress, assessing your efforts, and making necessary adjustments. Holding yourself accountable to your plan increases your chances of staying disciplined and achieving your goals.

3. **Motivation and Resilience**: A personal discipline plan can also be a source of motivation and resilience. Regularly reviewing your plan and reflecting on your progress

reinforces your commitment to your goals and reminds you of the reasons behind your efforts. This can help you stay motivated even when challenges arise.

Creating a personal discipline plan involves several key components, each of which plays a crucial role in helping you stay disciplined and achieve your goals. Let's explore these components in detail:

1. **Goal Setting**: Your goals are the foundation of your discipline plan. Start by identifying your long-term objectives—what you want to achieve in various areas of your life, such as career, health, relationships, personal development, and finances. Once you've defined your long-term goals, break them into smaller, more manageable short-term goals or milestones. These smaller goals will serve as stepping stones toward your larger objectives, making the process more achievable and less overwhelming.

When setting goals, use the SMART criteria (Specific, Measurable, Achievable, Relevant, Time-bound) to ensure that your goals are clear, realistic, and actionable. For example, instead of setting a vague goal like "improve my health," you might set a SMART goal like "lose 10 pounds in three months by exercising four times a week and following a balanced diet."

2. **Prioritization**: Once you have your goals, the next step is to prioritize them. Not all goals are equally important; some require more immediate attention than others. Prioritization helps you focus your time and energy on the tasks impacting your long-term success.

Use tools like the Eisenhower Matrix or the ABCDE Method to categorize and prioritize your tasks. This will help you stay focused on your most important goals and avoid getting sidetracked by less critical activities.

3. **Time Management**: Effective time management is essential for maintaining discipline. Your discipline plan should include a time management strategy that helps you allocate your time efficiently and stay organized. Techniques like time blocking, the Pomodoro Technique, and the Two-Minute Rule can be incorporated into your plan to help you make the most of your time.

Create a daily or weekly schedule with dedicated time for your most important tasks and goals. Be realistic about how much time each task will take and build in buffer time for unexpected interruptions or delays. Regularly review and adjust your schedule to align with your priorities and goals.

4. **Habit Formation**: Discipline is often driven by habits—consistent behaviors that become automatic over time. Your personal discipline plan should include a strategy for building and reinforcing positive habits that support your goals. This might involve creating new habits or modifying existing ones.

Start by identifying the critical habits that will help you achieve your goals. For example, if your goal is to improve your physical fitness, the essential habits include daily exercise, healthy eating, and getting enough sleep. Use techniques like habit stacking, linking a new habit to an existing one, or the cue-routine-reward framework to establish and reinforce these habits.

Track your habits regularly to monitor your progress and make adjustments as needed. Celebrating small wins and milestones can also help reinforce positive habits and motivate you.

5. **Overcoming Obstacles**: No plan is without challenges, and anticipating potential obstacles is crucial to maintaining discipline. Your discipline plan should include a strategy for identifying and overcoming the challenges that are most likely to arise.

Start by reflecting on the common challenges you've faced, such as procrastination, distractions, or self-doubt. Then, develop strategies to address these challenges when they occur. For example, if procrastination is a recurring issue, you might implement the Pomodoro Technique to help you stay focused and break tasks into manageable chunks.

Additionally, consider how you will handle setbacks and failures. Develop a mindset that views challenges as opportunities for growth and create a plan for bouncing back quickly when things don't go as planned.

6. **Accountability and Support**: Accountability is a critical factor in maintaining long-term discipline. Your discipline plan should include a strategy for holding yourself accountable and seeking support from others when needed.

Consider sharing your goals with a trusted friend, mentor, or accountability partner who can provide encouragement, feedback, and motivation. Regular check-ins with your accountability partner can help you stay on track and adjust as needed. Alternatively, you might join a support group or community of like-minded individuals working toward similar goals.

In addition to external accountability, practice self-accountability by regularly reviewing your discipline plan and tracking your progress. Use a journal or planner to document your achievements, challenges, and reflections. This practice will help you stay focused, motivated, and aligned with your goals.

7. **Mindset and Motivation**: Sustaining discipline over the long term requires a strong mindset and a deep sense of motivation. Your discipline plan should include cultivating a positive, growth-oriented mindset and maintaining motivation.

Techniques like visualization, affirmations, and mindfulness can help you stay focused on your goals and maintain a positive outlook, even when faced with challenges. Regularly revisit your "why"—the deeper reasons behind your goals—and use it as a motivation to keep going.

Additionally, practice self-compassion and resilience. Recognize that setbacks are a natural part of the journey and treat yourself with kindness and understanding when things don't go as planned. By maintaining a positive and resilient mindset, you can sustain your discipline and continue making progress toward your goals.

8. **Review and Adaptation**: Finally, your personal discipline plan should be a living document that evolves as you grow and change. Review your plan regularly to assess your progress, reflect on what's working and what's not, and make adjustments as needed.

Set aside weekly or monthly time to review your goals, habits, and strategies. Celebrate your successes, identify areas for improvement, and adapt your plan to reflect any changes in your circumstances or priorities. This ongoing process of review and adaptation will help you stay aligned with your goals and ensure that your discipline plan continues to serve you effectively.

Creating a personal discipline plan is a decisive step toward achieving your long-term goals and maintaining the discipline needed for sustained success. By setting clear goals, prioritizing your time, building positive habits, overcoming obstacles, and staying accountable, you can create a roadmap that guides you through life's challenges and opportunities.

Remember that discipline is not a one-time effort but a continuous process of growth and improvement. Your discipline plan is a tool that will evolve with you, helping you stay focused, motivated, and resilient as you work toward your aspirations.

As you progress with your personal discipline plan, embrace the journey with confidence and commitment. The path to success is rarely linear, but with discipline, determination, and the right strategies, you can achieve your goals and create the life you envision.

As we conclude this book, reflecting on our journey through the various aspects of discipline is essential. Each chapter has been a building block, contributing to a comprehensive understanding of how discipline shapes success and how you can cultivate and sustain it. Whether your goals are personal, professional, or a combination of both, discipline is the thread that weaves together the fabric of achievement, resilience, and long-term fulfillment.

Chapter 1 laid the groundwork by exploring what discipline truly means. Discipline is not just about rigid self-control or forcing yourself to work; it's about making consistent, intentional choices that align with your long-term goals and values. Understanding the psychology of discipline helps interpret it, revealing that discipline is a skill that can be developed by anyone, regardless of their starting point. We debunked myths that discipline is innate or requires constant willpower, emphasizing instead that it's a habit that grows stronger with practice.

Discipline is the cornerstone of success. It bridges the gap between ambitions and accomplishments. The key takeaway from the foundational chapters is that discipline is not a one-time effort but a sustained practice that requires clear goals, consistent effort, and the ability to overcome obstacles.

THE ROLE OF PSYCHOLOGY AND HABIT FORMATION

Chapters 2 and 4 delved deeper into the psychology of self-discipline and the science of habit formation. These chapters highlighted how our brains work about habits and self-control, emphasizing the importance of understanding triggers, routines, and rewards. Habits are powerful because they operate mainly on autopilot, reducing the need for conscious effort and willpower. By forming positive habits and breaking negative ones, you can make disciplined behavior almost automatic.

The discussion on habit formation underscored the importance of starting small, being consistent, and using techniques like habit stacking and tracking progress. These strategies help reinforce discipline by embedding it into your daily routines. The key to long-term success lies in building a solid foundation of habits that support your goals, making discipline a natural part of your life rather than a constant struggle.

Chapters 5 and 6 focused on overcoming two of the most common barriers to discipline: procrastination and distractions. Procrastination is a universal challenge that often stems from deeper psychological factors such as fear of failure, perfectionism, or lack of motivation. We explored practical strategies to combat procrastination, including breaking tasks into smaller steps, setting specific deadlines, and using techniques like the Pomodoro Technique to maintain focus.

Distractions, particularly in today's digital age, are another significant obstacle to maintaining discipline. We examined the impact of distractions on productivity and explored ways to minimize them, such as creating a dedicated workspace, using time blocking, and practicing mindfulness. Managing distractions is crucial for staying focused on your goals and maintaining the discipline needed to achieve them.

These chapters reinforced that discipline is not about willpower alone but about creating an environment and mindset supporting sustained focus and effort. By addressing procrastination and distractions head-on, you can remove the obstacles to your success.

SUSTAINING DISCIPLINE OVER THE LONG TERM

Chapters 7 and 9 tackled sustaining discipline over the long term. Mental toughness emerged as a critical theme, highlighting the importance of resilience, confidence, and emotional regulation in maintaining discipline. Developing mental toughness allows you to persevere through setbacks, maintain focus under pressure, and stay committed to your goals even when motivation decreases.

Sustaining discipline requires more than initial effort; it demands ongoing commitment, adaptability, and overcoming challenges like burnout, loss of motivation, and complacency. We discussed the importance of setting realistic and flexible goals, incorporating rest and recovery, and celebrating progress rather than perfection. These strategies help ensure that discipline is not just a short-term burst of effort but a sustained practice that leads to lasting success.

TIME MANAGEMENT AND PRIORITIZATION

Chapter 8 discusses time management and prioritization, which are critical components of sustaining discipline. Effective time management allows you to focus on what truly matters, avoid unnecessary stress, and create a sense of control over your daily life. Techniques like the Eisenhower Matrix, Time Blocking, and the Pomodoro Technique provide practical tools for managing your time efficiently and staying organized.

Prioritization involves making intentional choices regarding where to direct your time and energy. You can make meaningful progress toward your objectives by aligning your tasks with your long-term goals and prioritizing the most critical activities. Time management and prioritization are not just about doing more; they're about doing what matters most, which is essential for maintaining discipline over the long term.

CREATING A PERSONAL DISCIPLINE PLAN

Finally, in Chapter 10, we combined all the concepts and strategies discussed throughout the book into a comprehensive personal discipline plan. This plan serves as your roadmap for maintaining discipline and achieving your goals. By setting clear, actionable goals, prioritizing your tasks, building positive habits, and staying accountable, you create a structured approach to discipline tailored to your unique needs and aspirations.

Your personal discipline plan is a living document that evolves with you. It's not static; it requires regular review, reflection, and adjustment. Your plan should adapt as you grow, and your circumstances change to continue serving you effectively. The plan is a tool to keep you focused, motivated, and resilient as you navigate the challenges and opportunities on your path to success.

THE POWER OF DISCIPLINE IN ACHIEVING SUCCESS

It's essential to recognize the transformative power of discipline. Discipline is not about deprivation or rigid control; it's about empowerment and the ability to shape your life according to your values and goals. It's the foundation upon which all success is built, enabling you to turn your dreams into reality through consistent, purposeful action.

The road to success is rarely smooth, and challenges are inevitable. However, with discipline, you have the tools to navigate these challenges, stay focused on your goals, and persevere even when the going gets tough. The strategies and insights shared in this book are designed to help you build and sustain the discipline needed to achieve your full potential.

Remember that discipline is a journey, not a destination. It's a continuous process of growth, learning, and self-improvement. By embracing discipline as a way of life, you can create lasting change, achieve your most ambitious goals, and experience the fulfillment that comes from living in alignment with your true purpose.

As you move forward, apply the lessons from this book in your daily life. Use your discipline plan as a guide but remain open to learning and adapting as you grow. With discipline as your foundation, there is no limit to what you can achieve.

Dr. Clement Kwakye is not just another voice in the crowded world of personal development—he's a trusted expert whose techniques and insights have transformed the lives of countless individuals seeking real and lasting change. With a Ph.D. in Education and advanced training in leadership coaching, Dr. Kwakye has spent years honing his craft, blending academic rigor with practical, hands-on strategies that deliver tangible results. His passion for unlocking human potential has solidified his reputation as a leader in life coaching and personal development.

Through years of dedicated practice, teaching, and mentorship, Dr. Kwakye has become a guiding light for individuals seeking to break through personal and professional barriers. His expertise in discipline strategies has empowered clients from all walks of life to achieve more than they ever thought possible. Whether it's helping professionals reach the next level in their careers or guiding individuals toward personal breakthroughs, techniques offered in this book go beyond surface-level motivation—they drive deep, lasting transformation.

At the heart of his coaching program, *Mastering Discipline for Personal and Professional Success* is the core principle that discipline isn't just about rules or restrictions—it's about creating a mindset of self-mastery that touches every part of your life. Dr. Kwakye doesn't just teach discipline; he lives and breathes it. His unique approach ensures that clients learn new habits and internalize them, applying these strategies consistently to achieve their most ambitious goals.

This book is built on the philosophy that true transformation doesn't happen overnight. It takes time, commitment, and the right guidance. His techniques empower individuals to ignite and sustain their motivation over the long term, fostering resilience, focus, and a relentless drive toward success.

What sets Dr. Kwakye apart is his ability to instill discipline in a way that feels empowering, not restrictive. His clients don't just leave with a list of strategies; they walk away with a profound understanding of how to implement discipline in their daily lives— whether that's in their careers, personal lives, or relationships. The results? A powerful and engaging experience that continues to deliver value long after the coaching sessions have ended.

Dr. Kwakye has become a beacon for those ready to commit to lasting growth, offering them not only the strategies to succeed but the mindset to sustain that success for years to come.

If you're ready to experience this level of transformation, Dr. Kwakye is here to guide you on the journey. Prepare to unlock your potential, overcome your obstacles, and master the discipline that leads to unparalleled personal and professional success.

Ckprofessionalconsulting@gmail.com

www.ingramcontent.com/pod-product-compliance
Lightning Source LLC
Chambersburg PA
CBHW051542120626
46551CB00013B/1339